Abracada|

C000056404

FLUTE

TECHNIQUE

Building solid foundations and technical skills

Malcolm Pollock

A & C BLACK
AN IMPRINT OF BLOOMSBURY
LONDON NEW DELHI NEW YORK SYDNEY

Contents

Getting started

This section guides you through the basics of setting up and looking after your flute, posture, hand position and how to practise. Get these right and you'll be off to a great start!

Putting your flute together

✻ Use the pictures below (a or b) to identify each part of your flute and to see how the parts fit together.

a) Straight head joint flute:

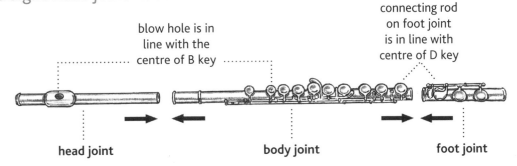

blow hole is in line with the centre of B key

connecting rod on foot joint is in line with centre of D key

head joint   body joint   foot joint

b) Curved head joint flute:

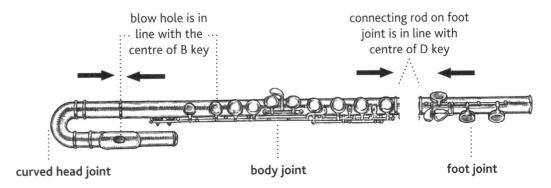

blow hole is in line with the centre of B key

connecting rod on foot joint is in line with centre of D key

curved head joint   body joint   foot joint

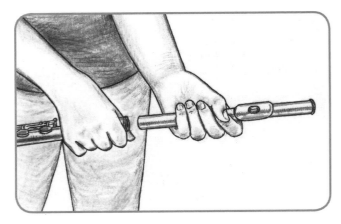

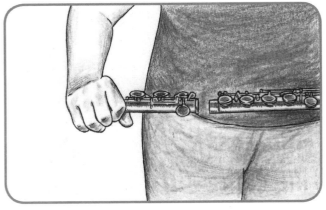

1. Gently push and twist the head joint onto the body joint to slot them together. Don't grip the keys as they can easily be damaged.

2. Repeat the same action and slot the foot joint into the main body.

Holding your flute

✴ Your flute needs to be balanced in three places:

- your bottom lip and chin;
- the lower joint of your left index finger;
- your right thumb.

✴ Left hand:

fingers in the centre of
each key and slightly curved

flute resting on
the lower joint of
your index finger

little finger reaches
the G sharp key
comfortably

top joint of your
straight thumb on
the long key at the
back of the flute

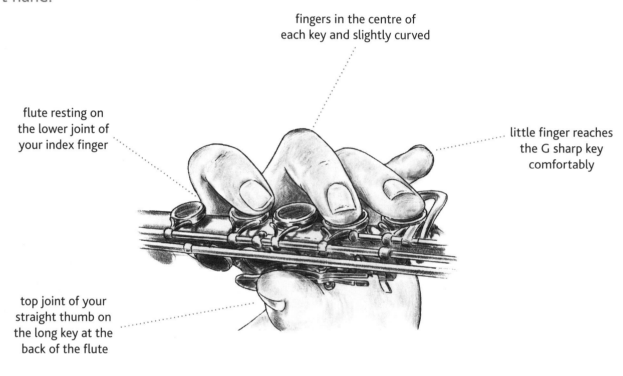

✴ Right hand:

relax your hand
and don't grip
tightly

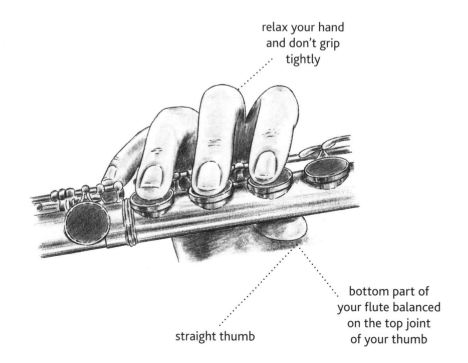

bottom part of
your flute balanced
on the top joint
of your thumb

straight thumb

Standing posture

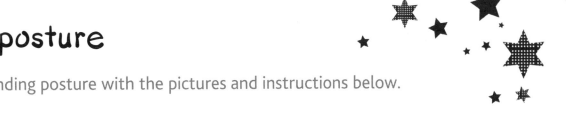

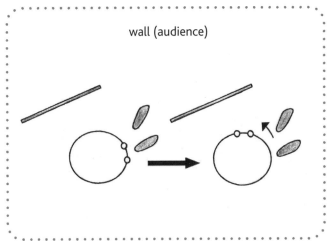

1. Put your flute down on a flat surface.

2. Standing opposite a wall (your audience), adjust your music stand so that it is slightly to your left and slightly lower than eye level.

3. Pick up your flute. Postion your feet at a 2 o'clock position in relation to the wall with your left foot slightly in front of the right.

4. Without moving your feet, turn your upper body to the left so that you are facing the wall.

5. Position your fingers on the keys using the pictures opposite. Bring the flute to your bottom lip.

flute slightly lower than horizontal

shoulders and neck relaxed

straight back

elbows not too high or too low

left foot slightly in front of the right foot

feet slightly apart

TOP TIP!

Try not to sway when you play as any movements will affect your sound.

6. Your flute should be parallel with the wall and slightly lower than horizontal. Your shoulders should be relaxed and not lifted.

Sitting posture

✴ You will usually need to sit down when playing in a group. You may also prefer to sit down while you practise.

✴ Check your sitting posture with the picture below.

shoulders and
neck relaxed

straight back

flute slightly lower
than horizontal

don't rest your arm on
the back of the chair

sit towards the
front of the chair

legs slightly apart

feet flat
on the floor

Cleaning your flute

1. Use a cleaning rod and lint-free cloth to clean the inside of your flute before you put it away.

2. Make sure the rod is covered by the cloth to stop the insides of your flute getting scratched.

3. Be careful not to force the rod down your flute, especially when you're cleaning the head joint.

Putting your flute away

✳ Use the picture below to see how your flute should look in its case.

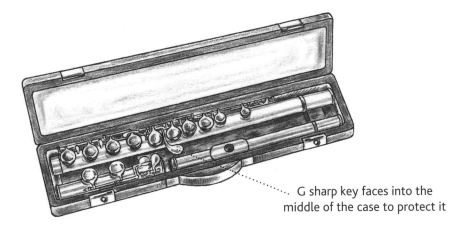

G sharp key faces into the middle of the case to protect it

Transporting your flute

✳ Don't keep anything except for your flute in the case. Putting things like the cleaning cloth or your music in the case will damage the keys.

✳ Instead, put the cleaning rod and cloth in the side pocket of a soft carry case and use a music bag for your music.

Practice tips

- Check that your flute is lined up properly (see page 3).
- Check your posture and finger positions against the pictures on pages 4–6.
- Practise little and often (no more than ten or fifteen minutes to start with).
- Don't practise if you feel too tired.
- Use warm-ups to start your sessions.
- Practise the difficult bits as well as the easy bits.
- Play your pieces slowly at first, then speed up as you get better.

Part 1: Sound

This section covers all the things that will improve the sound you make – from the way you position the flute on your lip, to the shape you make with your mouth, and your breathing technique.

Embouchure

✶ The shape that your mouth makes when you play the flute is called the **embouchure** (pronounced *om-boo-shore*).

Embouchure activity

- For this activity you will only need your head joint.
- Stand in front of a mirror and use the picture and the four steps below to see where the mouthpiece should go on your lip.

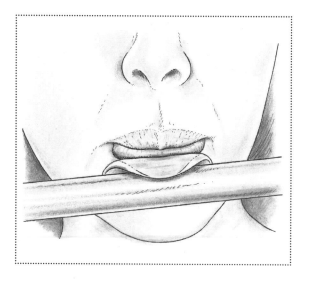

1. Place the lip plate on your bottom lip. The blow hole should be placed centrally on your lip.

2. Make sure that your bottom lip is covering about a third of the blow hole.

3. Slightly stretch your bottom lip at each end and make a small hole between your lips. The hole should be in the centre of your lips.

4. Breath in, then blow across the hole, keeping the same embouchure position.

Breathing

⭐ Practise the activities below regularly to improve your breath control so that you have enough air to make a strong sound and to get through longer phrases.

• Standing up straight, put both hands on your tummy, just below your ribs.

• Yawn, opening your mouth widely, then follow the instructions below:

Breathing in:

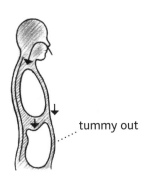

tummy out

1. Breathe in through your mouth for four counts, just as you did when you yawned. You should feel your tummy and chest getting bigger.

2. Try to relax your throat and shoulders as if you were saying 'ahhhhh' and breathe as quietly as possible.

3. Make the embouchure on page 8.

Breathing out:

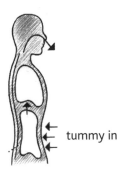

tummy in

4. Gently tighten your tummy muscles in and breathe out for four counts. You should feel your tummy and chest getting smaller.

5. Check that your throat and shoulders are still relaxed.

⭐ How did you get on? It takes time to develop breath control so keep practising regularly!

 ## Big breath challenge

• Hold a strip of paper against a wall and blow onto it using the embouchure on page 8.

• Now take your hand away. Can you stop the paper falling down? How long can you do this for? Use a stopwatch and compare your times with your friends.

• Try breathing out in this way while you make a sound with your head joint.

Making a sound

⁎ Put your flute together using the pictures on page 3 to check that the joints are lined up correctly.

⁎ Use a mirror to check your embouchure against the picture on page 8 and adjust it if necessary.

1 Beautiful

⁎ Listen carefully to your playing and try to make a full sound on each note, breathing during the rests.

Moderato   MP

⁎ TOP TIP!
If the notes sound too 'breathy' make sure the hole between your lips is not too big.

⁎ TOP TIP!
Try to memorise these pieces so that you can check your posture and embouchure in a mirror while you play them.

2 Three blind mice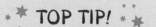

Very slowly   traditional

⁎ Did you move your fingers without any 'bumps'?

⁎ Did your As and Gs sound as good as your Bs?

3 Smoothies

Slowly and expressively   MP

⁎ Did your Cs sound as good as the rest of the notes? Play some long Bs and long Cs to compare them.

Tone

✳ The sound you make on the flute is also called the tone.

✳ To make a good tone, you need to make the embouchure on page 8 and use the breathing technique on page 9.

4 Home straight ③

✳ Check that you have a good tone for the C, then spread the sound to the other notes.

✳ Make sure that you are using the fleshy parts of your fingers on the middle of the keys.

CH

5 Gliding

✳ Make the notes before the breath marks (') slightly shorter to give yourself time to breathe.

✳ Listen carefully to check that you are moving smoothly between each note.

CH

✳ Did all of your notes have a strong and rounded tone?

✳ For a challenge, try breathing every four bars instead of every two bars.

✳ In future, try to work out where to breathe yourself, and put a comma or tick in the places you choose, to remind yourself.

Low notes

* To play **low notes**, you need to blow more air into the flute.

* Bring your **top lip forwards** slightly but don't tighten your lips too much. Use your tummy muscles to keep the air flowing constantly down the flute (think back to the *Big breath challenge* on page 9).

6 Lounging low

* Check that you have a good tone for the G, then spread the sound to the other notes.

* Start by practising two bars at a time.

CH

TOP TIP!

Ask your teacher to check that the key pads on your flute are not leaking as this can affect your sound.

7 Alice the camel

traditional

Moving up

✳ To play higher notes, you need blow the air faster through the flute.

✳ As you get higher, gradually push more and more with your tummy muscles to support the airflow. Make sure your embouchure stays steady while you're doing this.

8 Moving up

✳ Practise without the slurs at first if you find them difficult.

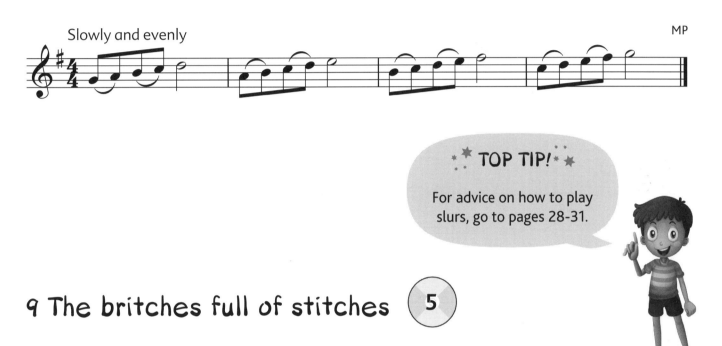

> ✳ TOP TIP! ✳
>
> For advice on how to play slurs, go to pages 28-31.

9 The britches full of stitches   ⑤

✳ Start by practising one line at a time.

✳ Make sure you move smoothly from one note to the next.

Intervals

* The distance between two notes is called an interval.

* For **larger intervals** you need to adjust your embouchure more and vary the speed that the air moves through the flute.

10 Riding west (6)

* Keep your lips flexible, particularly when playing larger intervals.

CH

> **TOP TIP!**
>
> Practise without the slurs to start with, then gradually add them in.

11 Sky lantern (7)

CH

Playing quietly (*piano*)

* To play quietly (*piano*), move your jaw **forwards** slightly so less air goes down the flute.

* Support the airflow with your tummy muscles.

Piano embouchure activity

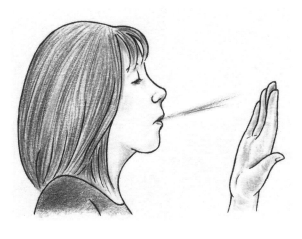

1. Make the embouchure on page 8 and blow directly into the palm of your hand. Support the airflow with your tummy muscles to keep your blowing smooth and constant.

2. Bring your jaw forwards slightly, keeping the embouchure tight. Can you feel the air moving up your middle finger?

3. Make sure you only move your jaw, and keep your head, hands and flute still.

4. Try playing a few quiet notes with your head joint using the same *piano* embouchure.

12 Souallé

* Play smoothly and quietly, imagining that you are trying to send a baby to sleep.

Andante

African

13 Who will buy? 8

Lionel Bart

15

Playing quietly on higher notes

14 The old letter

⁎ For **larger intervals** like D to A, slightly tighten your lips and blow a little harder as you play the **higher** notes.

CH

⁎ **TOP TIP!** ⁎
Remember to take your top lip backwards slightly, and support more with your tummy muscles when playing higher notes.

15 Durme, durme

⁎ Play this piece as smoothly and quietly as possible, even though the notes are quite high.

16

Playing loudly (*forte*)

✳ To play **loudly** (*forte*), move your jaw **backwards** slightly so more air goes through the flute.

✳ Support the airflow with your tummy muscles.

Forte embouchure activity

1. Make the embouchure on page 8 and blow directly into the palm of your hand. Support the airflow with your tummy muscles to stay in tune.

2. Bring your jaw backwards slightly, keeping the embouchure tight. Can you feel the air moving down from your palm to your arm?

3. Make sure you only move your jaw, and keep your head, hands and flute still.

4. Try the *forte* embouchure with your head joint.

16 Ode to joy

✳ Try to make a strong tone on all the notes but don't blow too hard!

Ludwig van Beethoven

17 Sweet home Chicago (10)

Driving blues

traditional

✳ Did your Es sound as strong as the other notes?

Playing loudly on higher notes

18 Steeple bells (11)

✳ Spread the good tone from the high G down to the lower notes.

✳ Put your fingers down smoothly on the keys when changing notes.

traditional

19 The jolly pirate (12)

✴ Take lots of breath at the beginning of this piece, and make sure you top up in the rests!

CH

⁎˙⁎ TOP TIP! ⁎˙⁎

Start by practising slowly, then gradually increase the speed.

20 Wake up!

✴ Make sure you start each note clearly and crisply (see page 24 for advice on tonguing).

traditional

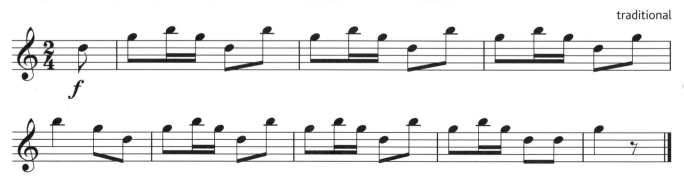

Loud to quiet (*diminuendo*)

* When we play loudly then gradually get quieter, it is called a *diminuendo*.

* Move your jaw forwards gradually (see page 15) and keep blowing the same amount of air down the flute. Don't forget to support the airflow with your tummy muscles.

21 Diminuendo (13)

* Can you make the biggest possible difference between the volume at the beginning and the end of each note, but also make the change smoothly and evenly?

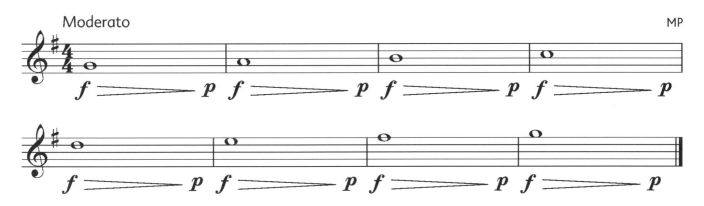

* If you are finding this piece tricky, try playing each note *forte*, then start the same note again and play it *piano*. Then try the *diminuendos* again.

TOP TIP!

Listen carefully to your tuning, especially at the ends of phrases. Support the airflow more with your tummy muscles if your notes are sounding flat.

22 Feed the birds (14)

* Make sure your sound is clear all the way through the *diminuendos*.

* For each note, keep the air going through the flute at the same speed whatever dynamic you are playing.

Robert and Richard Sherman

Quiet to loud (*crescendo*)

* When we play quietly then gradually get louder it is called a *crescendo*.

* Move your jaw backwards gradually (see page 17) being careful not to overblow as it will affect the tuning. Don't forget to support the airflow with your tummy muscles.

23 Tiny tango

* Make sure the rhythms here are crisp, and that you use your tongue well (see page 24 for advice on tonguing).

CH

24 Song of the Volga boatmen

* Try to *crescendo* right to the end of the phrase without the notes getting too sharp!

Slowly

Russian

20

Playing quietly and loudly

✳ When you are playing a piece with both loud (*forte*) **and** quiet (*piano*) notes, you will need to adjust your embouchure using the jaw movements on pages 15 and 17.

✳ Don't forget to support the airflow with your tummy muscles and keep the same air speed for each note, no matter how quietly or loudly you play.

25 At a canter (16)

✳ Try to make the difference between the *fortes* and the *pianos* as obvious as possible.

✳ Listen carefully to your tuning and adjust your embouchure if you need to.

CH

26 Beauty and the beast (17)

✳ Make sure you make a real difference between the louds and softs, and in particular make sure you *diminuendo* evenly.

Howard Ashman and Alan Menken

Review: sound

❋ These pieces bring together all of the techniques that you have learnt in the **Sound section**.

27 Edelweiss

Richard Rodgers and Oscar Hammerstein

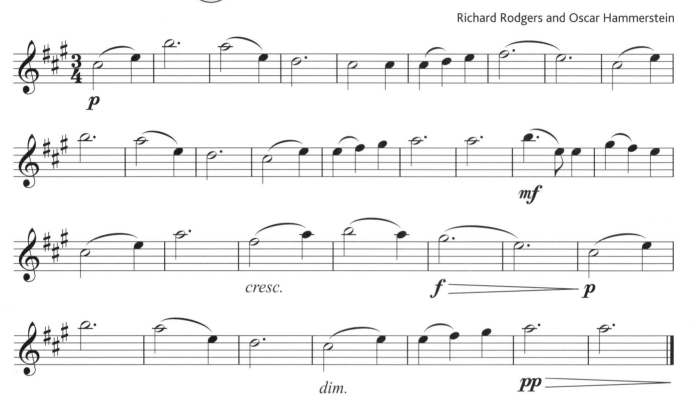

28 Lord of the dance

❋ Play with a strong, even tone, taking care not to blow too hard on the top notes.

29 Love walked in

George and Ira Gershwin

Part 2: Articulation

Articulation means starting notes cleanly so that each one can be heard clearly. This section helps you to build up your tongue and tummy muscles to improve your articulation.

Tonguing

✳ To **articulate** you need to use your **tongue** to start the notes clearly and cleanly.

✳ The **tip** of your tongue should quickly touch the **back of your top front teeth** as if you were saying 't'.

Tonguing activity

1. Stand in front of a mirror with the palm of your hand a few centimetres in front of your mouth.

2. Take a deep breath then breathe out using your flute embouchure, and touch the back of your top front teeth quickly with the end of your tongue. Try to imagine you are spitting out a grain of rice stuck between your lips!

3. Make sure your embouchure doesn't change shape.

4. Can you feel the airflow stopping and starting on your hand?

5. Next, try tonguing some notes with the flute head joint.

30 Raindrops ⑲

Using your tummy muscles

✳ You also need to use your **tummy muscles** to support the airflow when you tongue.

✳ Your tummy muscles help to push the air out quickly to make a clearer sound.

Tummy articulation activity

1. Take a deep breath, then make the embouchure on page 8.

2. Blow out four short puffs without taking a breath in between each one. Each time you blow out, give a little push with your tummy muscles as if you are blowing out candles.

3. Make sure your embouchure doesn't change shape and your throat and neck are relaxed.

31 Gloriantur (20)

✳ No tonguing allowed for this piece! Use only your tummy muscles to push the air out for each note.

Carl Orff

32 On tiptoes (21)

✳ Use your tummy muscles and your tongue **together** for this piece.

✳ Use your tongue to start the note cleanly.

CH

25

Linked together tonguing (*legato*)

✳ *Legato* is an Italian word that means **'linked together'**.

✳ To tongue *legato* notes, the air stream needs to be continuous (as if you were slurring). Don't forget to support the airflow with your tummy muscles (see pages 9 and 25).

33 Lonely faces 22

✳ Make this tune sound as expressive and smooth as you can.

✳ Try to think of each note as part of one long phrase.

CH

34 Moanin'

✳ Always tongue with a **light touch**, however loudly you are playing.

✳ As this is a jazz piece, the rhythms can be swung.

Art Blakey

Detached tonguing (*staccato*)

* *Staccato* is an Italian word that means '**detached**'.

* *Staccato* notes should sound just as strong and clear as *legato* notes, except that they are shorter! Don't forget to support the airflow with your tummy muscles (see pages 9 and 25).

35 Step back 23

* Using your B flat thumb key may make this piece easier to play.

CH

36 We are dainty little fairies

* Make sure you move your tongue quickly on each note and keep your embouchure steady.

W.S. Gilbert and Arthur Sullivan

Slurring and tonguing

❋ Always tongue the first note of a slur and remember to keep blowing steadily through it.

37 Mumbai moonrise

❋ Always try to make the first note of a slur stronger and shorten the last note.

❋ Check you are balancing the flute correctly before you start this piece (see page 4).

38 Laughing all day

❋ Listen carefully as you play. Are the rhythms and tone as even as possible?

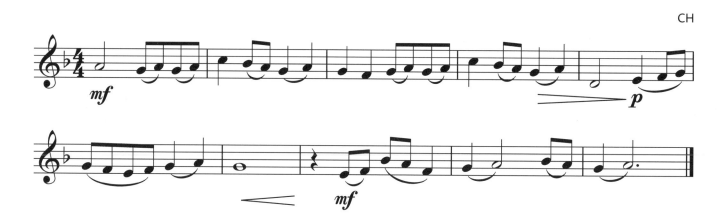

❋ Now go back to *The britches full of stitches* (page 13), *Who will buy?* (page 15), *Durme, durme* (page 16), *Song of the Volga boatmen* (page 20) and *Love walked in* (page 23) in Part 1: Sound, and try to make the articulation as clear as you can while still making a beautiful tone.

39 Parade 26

✴ Keep the rhythm as even as possible.

✴ Try to shorten the second note of the slur without rushing.

CH

40 Moscow nights

✴ Play with a strong, *legato* sound throughout.

✴ Try to make the contrast between the different dynamics as clear as possible.

Moderato

Russian

Slurring and tonguing (continued)

41 Caazapá

★ Check out your hand positions and balance points (see page 4) before you play this piece.

Andante

Agustín Barrios Mangoré

42 Can't hear any violins

* Always make sure that you are playing the slurs exactly as they are written.

CH

43 Can-can 28

* Play the *staccato* notes as lightly and evenly as possible.

* Make sure that you leave gaps between the *staccato* notes, and don't be tempted to speed up!

French

Faster tonguing

⁎ The tongue is a **muscle**. We have to build up its strength gradually before we can articulate **faster** notes.

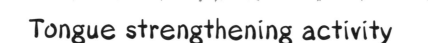

Tongue strengthening activity

1. Without your flute, breathe in deeply then make the embouchure shape on page 8.

2. Breathe out and tongue this pattern: TTT rest, TTT rest, BREATHE IN *(repeat pattern)*.

3. Touch your tongue lightly against your teeth in the same place each time.

4. Use the tip of your tongue and make small movements.

5. Repeat the pattern as much as you can and gradually get faster as your tongue gets stronger.

44 Saucy salsa 29

⁎ Remember to always move the tip of your tongue quickly and lightly, and always keep your embouchure steady.

45 Fanfare for five fair farmers 30

⁎ Keep your tongue as relaxed as possible: trying too hard will slow you down!

46 Chitty chitty bang bang

★ Push the air out with your tummy muscles on every two or
four notes (rather than on every note) when you play faster passages.

★ Remember to tongue as lightly as possible: if you try too hard, your tonguing will get slower!

Robert and Richard Sherman

Slow march time

47 In the hall of the mountain king 32

★ Check that your fingers and tongue are moving at the same speed!

★ Keep your fingers as close to the keys as possible (see page 4).

Edvard Grieg

Slow march time

D.C. repeat ad lib.

Fine

Faster tonguing (continued)

✴ Start with the activity on page 32 to wake your tongue up before you play these pieces!

48 Michael Finnegan

✴ Keep your lips still and your throat relaxed.

✴ Remember to tongue quietly and lightly even when you are playing *forte*.

traditional

49 Hazy habanera 〔33〕

✴ Make sure the dotted notes are long enough, and don't rush the semiquavers.

CH

Review: articulation

⭐ These pieces bring together all the techniques you have learnt in the **Articulation section**.

50 Song at sunrise

⭐ When you play slurs higher up on the flute it's even more important to have plenty of air and to support the sound with your tummy muscles.

CH

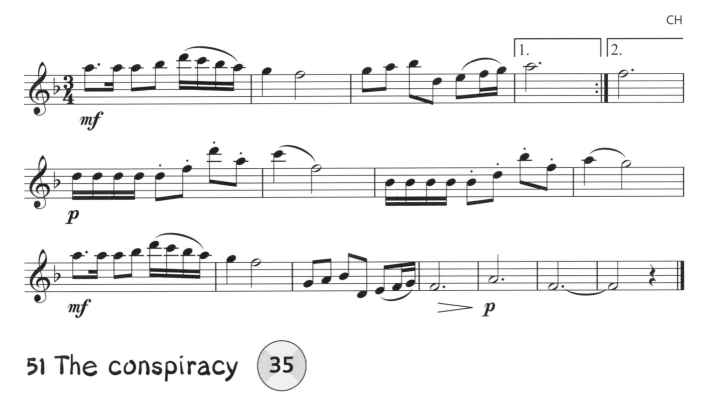

51 The conspiracy 35

⭐ Remember to work out where you are going to breathe before you start practising. You should draw a small tick or comma above the music to remind you where to breathe.

Irish

Part 3: Finger work

To play faster pieces on the flute, your hands and fingers need to be in the correct positions. You also need to train your fingers to move quickly and efficiently. This section will help you get the basic finger techniques right before moving onto more challenging, faster pieces.

Left hand finger work

★ The closer your fingers are to the keys, the quicker they will be able to move.

★ Practise these pieces in front of a mirror so that you can look at your fingers while you play. Keep checking your hand positions with the pictures on page 4.

52 Steps of Paris

★ Make sure your fingers are relaxed and close to the keys.

★ Practise each slur slowly and separately first, then put the piece together.

> ★ TOP TIP! ★
> If your left hand feels tense, shake it and then flop it back onto the keys.

53 Roll up! 37

★ Practise this slowly at first making sure your fingers are able to work evenly. Use the long B flat throughout.

Right hand finger work

✳ Slow down if your fingers are flapping around too much!

✳ Use a mirror to check your hand position is correct, and to make sure your fingers are close to the keys.

54 Little yellow wooden horse (38)

✳ Shake your right hand to relax it before you play this piece. Stop playing if you feel your hand tensing up.

CH

✳ Were your fingers close to the keys or were they moving about a lot?

> ✳ TOP TIP! ✳
> Play more slowly if your fingers are moving too much.

55 Sidewinder rock (39)

✳ Practise each bar separately first, making sure you can play the notes evenly.

✳ Make sure you use your right hand little finger for all the notes except bottom D.

CH

Scales

✹ Using your B flat thumb key throughout will make the F major scales easier.

56 A steady climb

CH

> **✦ TOP TIP! ✦**
> Keep the quavers as even as possible throughout this piece!

57 Minuet 41

✹ Try to change as evenly as possible from one note to the next,
especially when you have to move more than one finger at once.

J.S. Bach

58 Shoemaker's dance 42

★ Play slowly to start with, then build up the speed when your fingers are more familiar with the notes.

CH

59 The clockwork ballerina 43

★ Relax your fingers before you play this piece, and check your flute is balanced properly (see page 4).

CH

60 Breeze 44

★ Don't try to play this piece too fast, and make sure all of the semiquavers are even.

CH

Playing in flat keys

⭐ In general, pieces written in flat keys are a bit more difficult to play than those written in sharp keys. This is because the fingerings for B flats and E flats are harder than those for F sharps and C sharps.

61 Do re mi 45

⭐ It is fine to use your B flat thumb key when there are lots of B flats in a piece, but remember to look ahead and change back to the normal thumb key if you have to play B naturals.

Richard Rodgers and Oscar Hammerstein

62 Lenny the loafer 46

⭐ Check your hand positions before trying this piece, and make sure your flute is balanced (see page 4).

CH

40

Playing in sharp keys

Balance point hand activity

1. Kneel on a soft sofa to do this activity so that if you drop your flute it will fall onto the sofa, not the hard ground!

2. Finger a C sharp without blowing. Does the flute feel safe, or does it feel like you are going to drop it? If it feels wobbly go back to page 4 and check your three balance points.

3. When you are sure the flute is secure, practise playing a C sharp then a D.

63 Beneath the stars

* Check that you are holding your flute using the three balance points (see page 4).

* Does your tone sound even?

CH

64 Cradle song

* Make sure that you are balancing your flute well throughout this piece but be careful not to grip too hard!

Edvard Grieg

41

Arpeggios

★ *Arpeggio* is an Italian word than means 'played on a harp'.

★ Alongside scales, *arpeggios* are the other building blocks of most flute music.

65 The wizard prepares 49

★ Once again, use your B flat thumb key throughout this piece.

CH

66 Rocky ride 50

★ Make sure you play all the right notes in this piece: there are plenty of traps to fall into!

CH

67 March 51

★ Listen carefully as you play. Does your tone sound even?

68 Queen of Sheba backwards

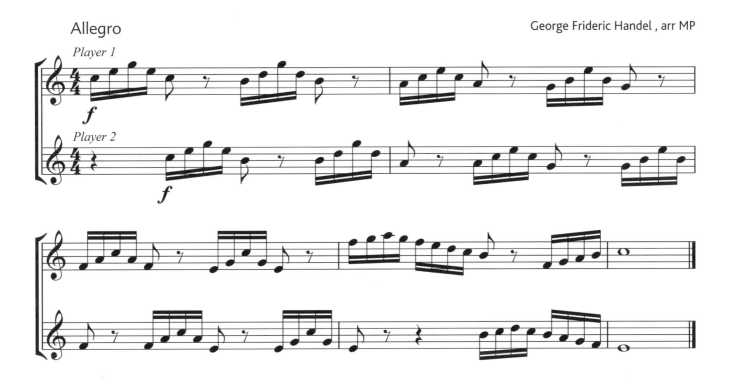

Allegro

George Frideric Handel , arr MP

69 Queen of Sheba the right way round!

✴ Practise this piece with and without your B flat thumb key.

George Frideric Handel

Allegro

Scales and arpeggios

✳ Most pieces have different combinations of scales and arpeggios like the pieces on the next few pages.

✳ Make sure you are playing the articulation as it is written in each piece.

70 Carnival calypso (52)

✳ Practise the arpeggios in bars 2, 4 and 6, before you try the whole piece.

CH

> **TOP TIP!**
> Where possible, try using different slurring and tonguing patterns, eg two notes slurred then two notes tongued, or slurring in groups of four.

71 Take a walk out of town (53)

✳ Practise very slowly at first and check that your fingers are working evenly.

CH

72 Chirpy charleston 54

✳ Really crisp tonguing is needed here, and make sure you don't rush!

CH

73 All that is wonderful 55

✳ Practise each bar separately to make sure you are playing the right notes.

CH

Scales and arpeggios (continued)

74 Rondeau

✳ Make sure you keep your fingers close to the keys so that you play the rhythms evenly,
  particularly the semiquavers.

Review: finger work

75 Torna a surriento

★ Slow music is also difficult for the fingers. Try to play this piece as smoothly as possible. Make sure no one can tell which are the difficult bits!

Ernesto De Curtis

Useful resources

Listen to as much flute music as possible so that you can explore what good flute playing sounds like (and what sort of sound you would like to make). Here is a short list of recordings and players you could start with:

Classical:

William Bennett: *Celebration for Flute and Orchestra* (ASV 1989) (Saint-Saëns *Romance*, Fauré *Fantaisie*).

Kenneth Smith: *Golden Flute* (ASV 1996) (Chaminade *Concertino*, Chopin *Variations*, Debussy *En Bateau*).

Emmanuel Pahud: *Vivaldi Flute Concertos* (EMI 2006) (No 3: *Il Gardellino*).

James Galway: *The Best of James Galway* (Sony 2009) (Rachmaninov *Vocalise*, Rimsky-Korsakov *Flight of the Bumble Bee*, James Horner *Titanic theme*).

Flute ensemble:

Quintessenz: *Tour de France* (Genuin 2007) (Prélude à l'après-midi d'un faune).

Irish traditional flute:

Steph Geremia: *The Open Road* (Black Box 2010) (The Conspiracy).

Kevin Crawford: *'D' flute* (Green Linnet 2006). (George White's Favourite, Dillon's Fancy).

Other folk flute music on YouTube or iTunes: panpipes, North American Indian flute, Japanese Shakuhachi.

Jazz flute:

Hubert Laws: *The Laws of Jazz* (Atlantic 2005) (All Soul, Bessie's Blues).

Gerald Beckett: *Flute Vibes* (Summit 2006) (The Soothsayer, FluteVibes).

Acknowledgements

The following have kindly granted permission for the inclusion of copyright material:

Beauty and the beast by Howard Ashman and Alan Menken, © 1991 Wonderland Music Company Inc. and Walt Disney Music Co. Ltd., Warner/Chappell Artemis Music Ltd. Reproduced by permission of Faber Music Ltd. All rights reserved.

Chitty chitty bang bang by Richard and Robert Sherman, and *Moanin'* by Art Blakey, used by permission of Music Sales Ltd. All rights reserved. International copyright secured.

Do re mi and *Edelweiss* by Oscar Hammerstein II and Richard Rodgers, © 1959 Oscar Hammerstein II and Richard Rodgers. This arrangement © 2014 by Williamson Music. Reprinted by permission of Hal Leonard Corporation.

Feed the birds by Richard and Robert Sherman, © 1964 Wonderland Music Company Inc., Warner/Chappell Artemis Music Ltd. Reproduced by permission of Faber Music Ltd. and Alfred Music Publishing Co. All rights reserved.

Gloriantur et letantur by Carl Orff, © 1937 Schott Music GmbH & Co. KG, Mainz. © renewed 1965. Reproduced by permission. All rights reserved.

Love walked in by George and Ira Gershwin. Reproduced by permission of Faber Music Ltd. All rights reserved.

Who will buy? by Lionel Bart, © 1960 Lakeview Music Publishing Co Ltd. Used by permission. All rights reserved.

All other original pieces and arrangements are copyright A&C Black Ltd. Every effort has been made to trace and acknowledge copyright owners. If any right has been omitted, the publishers offer their apologies and will rectify this in subsequent editions following notification.

Recording

Flute played by Hattie Jolly.

Backing tracks arranged by Christopher Hussey and programmed by Christopher Hussey and Jeremy Birchall.

Sound engineering by Stephen Chadwick, 3D Music Studio

50 Bedford Square, London, WC1B 3DP
www.bloomsbury.com/music
Bloomsbury is a registered trademark of Bloomsbury Publishing Plc
© 2015 A&C Black Ltd
ISBN 978-1-4081-9344-0

Illustrations by Ray and Corinne Burrows
Design by Inês Duarte
Music setting by David Weston
Edited by Flora Death, Michelle Daley, and Stephanie Matthews

Printed and bound in India by Replika Press Pvt Ltd